THE GOLDEN THREAD

D1599083

THE
GOLDEN THREAD

THE CONTINUITY OF ESOTERIC TEACHING

by
NATALIE N. BANKS

LUCIS PRESS LTD.
London

LUCIS PUBLISHING COMPANY
New York

COPYRIGHT © 1963 BY LUCIS TRUST

First Printing 1963

Fifth Printing 1999

ISBN No. 0-85330-127-1

Library of Congress Catalog Card Number: 99-76385

The Lucis Publishing Company is a non-profit organisation owned
by the Lucis Trust. No royalties are paid on this book.

This title is also available in Danish and Swedish.
Translation into other languages is proceeding.

LUCIS PUBLISHING COMPANY
120 Wall Street
New York, NY 10005

LUCIS PRESS, LTD.
Suite 54
3 Whitehall Court
London SW1A 2EF

MANUFACTURED IN THE UNITED KINGDOM
By Biddles Ltd., Guildford, Surrey

TABLE OF CONTENTS

A STORY FROM
GRECIAN MYTHOLOGY

Ariadne gave a ball of golden thread to Theseus to be unwound as he travelled through the tortuously winding paths of the gloomy labyrinth of Crete into which he had been sent by the King, ostensibly as a sacrifice, but in reality to slay the Minotaur which dwelt at its centre.

It was only by means of this gleaming thread held firmly throughout his terrifying journey that Theseus was able to return safely out of the dark and tangled maze—after slaying the Minotaur.

The King	Spirit.
Ariadne	Soul.
Theseus	Personality.
The Minotaur	Ignorance, Greed and Selfishness.
Labyrinth (its centre)	The darkest stage of the descent.
The Golden Thread.	The Teachings of the Ageless Wisdom.

LUCIS PUBLICATIONS

A number of these titles are referred to in this book.

CHAPTER ONE

THE GOLDEN THREAD

1. *The Continuity of Esoteric Teaching*

The constant reappearance of the Ancient or Ageless Wisdom, that body of inner or esoteric* teaching handed down from remote times in a form suitable to the period, has always attracted the minds of thoughtful people. Through its remarkable preservation and continuity it has been compared in symbol to a golden thread: a spiritual life-line waxing or waning in clarity and intensity from century to century.

Earth's first contact with the essence of this inner wisdom is thought to have taken place millions of years ago before any kind of record was possible. As described within the annals of the Ageless Wisdom the story of its inception and its development through many thousands of years is both instructive and inspiring and suggests the existence of both purpose and plan to all but the confirmed materialist or determined pessimist. To many there is strong evidence of design, a guarantee of wise guidance from behind the scenes, in spite of seeming evidence to the contrary when only short periods of time are considered.

Today in this transition period from the emotionally conditioned 2,160 years of the Piscean age of the Fishes into the mentally oriented age of Aquarius, Bearer of the Waters of Knowledge, we find many who are strongly attracted to the Ageless Wisdom but demand mental support for what they intuitively feel to be in line with truth. Such reasoned explanations are to be found through study of these occult* or esoteric teachings, which today can be understood in conjunction with the latest discoveries of science. These latter confirm the age-old occult teaching that all is energy at different levels of manifestation, and in this linking of the recent findings of science with the esoteric teaching, the mentally keen as well as the primarily intuitive seeker feels encouraged to investigate within the realms of esoteric science.

---

*The words "esoteric" and "occult" both mean hidden.

1

It is well to remember that statements from the Ageless Wisdom often arouse incredulity. They are, however, always inconclusive, since evolution is a continual process. They should be regarded as hypotheses until reading and thought reveal them first as possibilities, then as probabilities in the light of fuller knowledge and to some, in due course, as fact.

2.   *Some Sources of Information*

There is general agreement among students of the various branches of the Ageless Wisdom that from very ancient times there has existed a "root doctrine" comprising the basic laws and principles concerning the nature of Deity, the universe and man. Strong similarity between ideas on these fundamental subjects emerging at different periods and from widely separated localities tends to strengthen this view.

From opinions drawn from such well-known sources as *The Secret Doctrine* by H. P. Blavatsky, the many works of Mrs Annie Besant, the *Encyclopaedia of Secret Teachings* by Manly P. Hall and the Aquarian New Age teachings of "The Tibetan", written down at his dictation by Alice A. Bailey, we find the following:

We are told of a language, more ancient even than Sanskrit, called Senzar. It has no alphabet and consists of symbols—the interpretation of which is beyond the present development of the human mind. These symbols indicate the particular level and type of instruction suited to humanity during a given period. They are said to have been engraved on indestructible material and, with other similar documents, are kept in archives in the custody of the Great White Brotherhood. Guided by these records and their own wisdom those members of the Brotherhood who are specially in charge of human progress instigate the appearance of new ideas and teachings through all possible channels.

From translations by scholars and interpretations of the most ancient Vedas and puranas of India, from the Egyptian *Book of the Dead*, from other world scriptures, classical mythology, folklore and fable, a great fundamental body of truth with many branches is continually being discovered.

Architectural research also is constantly revealing new facets of the Ancient Wisdom, and through discoveries made in ancient ruins in Egypt, Peru, Mexico, Easter Island, Stonehenge and other places a great story of man's search for truth is unfolding itself. This is not only the story of outer physical man and his exploits, but also of his developing mind and his inner aspirations. These discoveries are of value to the occult student as he relates them to the different stages of man's evolving consciousness within the greater scheme of both planetary and cosmic life.

As we follow the golden thread of inner teaching we should note the sequential appearance of the different esoteric groups as being the specialised means of evoking the next faculty to be developed in an advanced minority, while the orthodox religions supply inspiration and guidance for the majority. In this manner men of all stages are drawn up from their own particular rung to the next as they steadily climb the ladder of evolution.

It is not possible in a short outline to attempt any recording of the founding of the world religions. Our intent is rather to follow the preservation and development of the truth that lies hidden within the outer teachings of them all.

3.   *The Teaching: Wholeness: the Underlying Theme*

Through the ideas and the ideals of the Ageless Wisdom the mind is immensely stimulated and begins noticeably to unfold its own unsuspected powers through the study of the nature and the amazing inter-relation of Deity, the solar system, planets and man. With the inclusion of every other kingdom of nature, a gradual realisation of wholeness is developed as well as a sense of proportion, both of which give a measure of perspective in the living of life and in dealing with its difficulties.

Obeying the age-old counsel "Man, know thyself, and thou shalt know the universe and God", and applying the laws of correspondence and analogy expressed in the maxim "As above, so below", we begin to understand the truth of the biblical saying that "Man is made in the image of God", that he is indeed a "God in the making".

Sages of the ancient east have long taught that the soul of each person overshadowed by spirit has become temporarily immersed in the material world so that through the experience of many lives on earth (reincarnation) each may develop his latent soul powers, thus obeying that rather perplexing command "Be ye therefore perfect, even as your Father in heaven is perfect". For man is still the prodigal son in a far country, though already on his return journey to his father's home with the assurance that "when afar off" he will be met and welcomed. Of this encouragement he becomes aware as soon as he truly tires of the "husks which the swine did eat". In increasing numbers humanity is now arriving at that very point of satiety, while quite a few are already long past it.

Belonging to any religion or to none and according to his stage of evolution, the seeker finds within the esoteric teachings of his day the means of understanding his spiritual and psychic self through meditation, study and service. It is in this manner, and after many lives of such experience, that the Elders of the human race have already reached that stage of relative perfection prescribed for us in every religion, its attainment being gradually achieved through the understanding of esoteric science and above all through living according to the teaching.

The logical outcome of such achievement is the existence of the Great White Brotherhood,* also called the Occult Hierarchy,* with its central council known as the Inner Government of the World.* Among its members are the great World Teachers such as the Christ and the Buddha and the Masters of Wisdom who are referred to in the scriptures as "Just men made perfect", of whom it is said that "they shall go no more out". This means that they have reached the stage where they do not need to reincarnate, though some choose to do so for humanity's benefit. These beings are the custodians of what is called "The Great Plan", which is part of a greater purpose (the Will of God). They lead and encourage the development of all esoteric teachings, they in fact preserve the existence and the continuity of the golden life-line, using all earthly channels available at any given time for spreading wisdom and knowledge in the manner in which humanity is best able to receive them.

*These three designations can be interchangeable and allude, generally speaking, to the same Body.

4. *The Founding on Earth of the Great White Brotherhood*

According to the ancient records this unique event oc-
curred some eighteen million years ago, about half-way through
the Lemurian Race, the Third Root Race of our own humanity.
It was at that time that the golden thread, the spiritual life-line
which was to continue through the ages, is said to have become,
as it were, anchored on earth by very advanced beings of an earlier race connected with the planet Venus, our elder sister planet, considered to be farther along the evolutionary path than
ourselves.

At that time humanity was polarised in the material or bod-
ily realms of existence, emotion being hardly present except in
those who were far advanced, while mentality was a quality for
the then distant future. During this far-off age, and until half-way
through the next Root Race, the Atlantean, the so-called Golden
Age of mythology, came very slowly into being. That was the time
when "gods walked with men"; for to the humanity of that early
period their highly evolved leaders appeared truly as "gods".

Very much later, and at a distinctly lower level, the same
God-man relationship was reflected in the "divine" priest-kings
of ancient Egypt, who before the decline of that country's greatness were far above the level of even their most advanced subjects. The symbolism of "the divine right of kings" comes down
from those distant days when spiritual development and merit
alone entitled a person to a position of great power. It is thought
that such inspired leadership will again become possible, for at
each turn of the evolutionary spiral humanity gradually devel-
ops its inner qualities of mind and soul sufficiently for the
Hierarchy again to walk with men.

Owing to the inspiring guidance and the deliberate incarnation of the greater ones among the people, a few Atlanteans
attained initiate level and in time joined the ranks of the Inner
Government of that far-off day. However, owing to a temporary
seizing of control by those known as "the dark brothers", the
Great White Lodge withdrew for a while from their close contact
with humanity, with the result that a large portion of the later
Atlantean race became a prey to the influence and actual use of
black magic (the selfish use of power). This gained entry and
operated through the people's low-grade emotional excesses,
which were stimulated by a very undeveloped mentality.

This terrible disaster, the nature of which we today can hardly imagine, led in time to the downfall of Atlantis when the whole continent was gradually submerged by a slow succession of floods; the last of these devastating upheavals being the great flood of the Old Testament, when the remaining island of Poseidonis was, according to Plato's description, swept away about the year 10,000 B.C.

Nevertheless, the golden thread of continuity was preserved; for before the final disaster a few advanced Atlanteans, led by the great teacher Hermes according to some occult writers, made good their escape and took the precious teachings into a remote fastness of central Asia.

CHAPTER TWO

FROM EAST TO WEST

1. *Egypt and the Ancient Mysteries*

According to the occult history of the ancient world, the preservation and transfer of the Ageless Wisdom teachings from Atlantis into central Asia came about in the following manner.

Before the last Atlantean cataclysm, described by Plato as the sinking of Poseidonis about 10,000 B.C., certain initiate survivors, bearing with them the Secret Doctrine teachings, had found their way into the seclusion of the Gobi Desert in central Asia. In esoteric literature we find the name "Shamballa" associated with this locality. In the inner teaching, Shamballa is considered to be a high state of consciousness within which the most advanced members of the Occult Hierarchy communicate with each other and impress their agents in any part of the world with instructions regarding the divine purpose and its working out on earth in what is known to esoteric students as "The Plan". For this work the earthly focus has been, and still is, this central Asian sanctuary, the home of "the one fundamental school of all occult teaching for our planet". (*Letters on Occult Meditation*, A. A. Bailey, p. 298.)

As the light of the sun rising in the east spreads slowly westwards, so has the light of wisdom travelled from this eastern land, which still preserves a few well guarded sanctuaries known only to senior members of the Great White Brotherhood, though many are the lesser ashrams controlled by teachers of various degrees of wisdom and knowledge and accessible to the serious traveller.

As we follow the course of the golden life-line of spiritual continuity flowing westward via Egypt and later through Arabia, the importance of this eastern source should be remembered, whether considered as a physical plane focus of spiritual teaching or as an inner plane centre and power house for the distribution of the light of the Ageless Wisdom to mankind.

The Ancient Mystery temples first established in Atlantis and continued in Egypt and later in Greece and Rome became the main repositories of esoteric teaching. Other centres of the

Mystery rites were those of Chaldea and Persia (from which arose the Mithraic cult), the Druidic Mysteries, celebrated in Britain and Gaul, and the Odinic rites of the Scandinavian and Germanic countries. There were also state Mysteries among the Inca, Maya and Aztec ancient civilisations. As Manly Hall (an author of valuable and extensive works on this subject) remarks, "No nation and age has been without its esoteric schools." Regarding the extreme importance of the Ancient Mysteries, the following opinion from another source is interesting. In his *General History of Freemasonry*, Robert Macoy writes:

"It appears that all the perfection of civilisation and all advancement made in philosophy, science and art among the ancients are due to those institutions which, under the veil of mystery, sought to illustrate the sublimest truths of religion, morality and virtue, and to impress them on the hearts of their disciples . . . their chief object was to teach the doctrine of the One God, the resurrection of man to eternal life, the dignity of the human soul; and to lead people to see the shadow of Deity in the beauty, magnificence and the splendour of the Universe."

The few Masons who today know something of the inner truths that Freemasonry has preserved and concealed see the craft as a faint far-off reflection of these Ancient Mystery temples and as a portent of their future return and expression at a higher level. The idea of the "restoration of the Mysteries" during the approaching Aquarian dispensation arises out of a deep intuitive realisation in the minds of some Masons and of many esoteric students of our own time, and is directly referred to and implied in a number of the Ageless Wisdom writings.

In time the Mysteries became perverted and their practices debased. Black Magic (selfish use of power) at first tainted and finally completely displaced White Magic. Bacchanalian orgies were introduced and a decline set in. But since these once mighty institutions contained the essence of truth, what was of value and was part of the plan for the spiritual growth of humanity was preserved for posterity.

Sun worship was fundamental to the teachings Egypt inherited from Atlantis and was later followed and also transformed by that great king Akhnaton into the first known monotheistic religion. Drama, ritual, chanting and rhythmic movement, as well as colourful processions for the people at festival times, all demonstrated different phases and modes of obeisance to the Solar Lord. There were also the ceremonies of lunar influence in relation to motherhood and the earth's fertility. These latter were remembered in what were known as the Mysteries of Isis in which women partook and served. Later, these rites bore the names of other goddesses.

Since the early religions had their origin in the northern hemisphere, the winter and summer solstices respectively marked the birth and beginning of the decline of the Sun-God for these ancient people. From this emerged in time a legend known as the "Dying God Myth". This was in reality no myth but a wonderful means of preserving knowledge of the beneficence of the cosmic principle, the sustaining life of our solar system, the Solar Logos. This "death and resurrection" has been repeatedly reflected down the ages by a succession of "Sun-Gods" said to have been born at the time of the first faint turning of darkness into light for the enlightenment of mankind, the last being the Lord Christ who many think will appear again near the beginning of the next century.

2. *The "One God Idea": Akhnaton and Moses*

Two outstanding contemporaries who sponsored the idea of the One God, and who were important links in strengthening the spiritual life-line of inner teaching, were King Akhnaton and the Prophet Moses. The latter is well known to students of the Old Testament, but recognition of the former is usually confined to the esoteric student and the Egyptologist. However, a strong persistence in human memory of an attempt that appeared to have failed can but indicate its underlying importance. Such is the case regarding the magnificent and inspired attempt of King Akhnaton of Egypt—a spiritual stand made by one man against the tremendous odds of a material and powerful priest-craft during the decline of Egypt's greatness.

A time link-up with biblical history is interesting: historical evidence, says Vera Reid in her fascinating and informative book *Towards Aquarius*, shows that the exodus of the children of Israel from the land of Egypt took place in the reign of Tutankhamen, indicating that Moses must have lived through the preceding

reign of King Amenhotep IV, who at that time called himself
Akhnaton or "Living in Truth". In this reign, says the same
author, "such a constant emphasis on truth has not been found
before or since". In this connection certain words from the
Cambridge History, Vol. II, are relevant.

"The modern world has yet to value this man who, in an era
so remote and under conditions so adverse, became the world's
first individual monotheist and first prophet of international-
ism, the most remarkable figure in the ancient world."

Religious reformation expressed in the One God idea
spread far and wide and influenced other national cults. From
Syria, Babylon and Persia word went forth forbidding the setting
up of graven images, and Mithra, formerly worshipped by the
Persians as the Sacred Bull, became "The Unconquerable Sun",
the slayer of the Bull. It is significant that at this time the sun was
moving out of the zodiacal sign of Taurus (the Bull) into the next
sign of Aries (the Ram); the forbidden worship of the golden calf
being an allusion to taking part in a form of worship belonging
to the past. Later, as again the sun's sign changed from Aries to
Pisces (the Fishes), the blood sacrifice of animals began very
slowly to lose its hold as the benign and compassionate influence
of the Christian teaching began to make itself felt.

3.   *Preparation for Approaching Darkness*

As if in preparation for the spiritual obscuration that was to
settle over all of Europe, a group of truly enlightened beings
appeared during the 600 years B.C. to establish certain aspects of
truth which the impending gloom was never able entirely to
obliterate. During this period came Pythagoras, Plato and a
number of followers of their schools. This was also the time of
the Lord Buddha, who was followed by such philosophers as
Laotze and Confucius; all leading up to the appearance, life and
teachings of Christ, which were to affect the world for the next
two thousand years and far beyond that time.

Moses and Pythagoras, and later Plato, were all thought to
have been in close contact with the true Ancient Mysteries and
to have been initiated in Egypt and India, thus deriving deep
occult knowledge through the eastern philosophy of the great
and ancient Indian sage Patanjali.

One could say that Pythagoras gave mental concept and numerical form to the older traditions; his system being based on music, mathematics, geometry and astronomy, from which he developed basic ideas on sound, rhythm and colour. The Ancient Mystery injunctions "Man know thyself" and "As above, so below" were used by Pythagoras to illustrate even more clearly than hitherto the wonderful relationship of Macrocosm and Microcosm (Universe and Man). He taught reincarnation but not transmigration* as has sometimes mistakenly been supposed.

The Pythagorean school at Crotona in southern Italy was conducted with very strict discipline and was divided into three grades. For the first two years at least the neophyte had to maintain complete silence. This was in training for the true silence or inner stillness which all great teachers deem essential for the perception of wisdom from intuitional levels as well as from mental concepts and from personal life experience.

4.   *The Dark Ages*

Such important events as the destruction of the Alexandrian libraries by fire and outstanding inventions such as that of the wheel and of printing have had a tremendous influence, both direct and indirect, on the spiritual development of mankind. The obvious effects have been either retarding or encouraging, but underlying every one of them has been the spur to human initiative; the fuel that drives the soul along the road to spiritual search and discovery. Such indeed was the deeper effect of the outwardly crushing limitations of mediaeval times.

While recognising the importance of historical events we must, however, in line with our objective, look within and see something of what took place under the cloak of darkness that spread over Europe in the Middle Ages, dimming the light of wisdom from the standpoint of esoteric teaching, yet without extinguishing the one persistent flicker, which is all we could now call the golden life-line of spiritual knowledge.

---

*Transmigration: the retrograde step of reincarnating in animal form after a human incarnation. Esoteric teaching considers this an impossibility.

Conditions during this period varied from time to time, but were mainly as follows: Universities were closed and learning in a proscribed form became confined within a narrow and powerful ecclesiastical hierarchy. Another conditioning factor of much misery, remote though it may seem, was the misinterpretation of Brahmanism that had arisen in India, strengthening the already very ancient caste system. This, with the negation of true Christianity in Europe, encouraged feudalism, a system with advantages for the few but full of inhumanity for the many. No tuition to lessen the harsh effects of this system, other than that permitted within the orthodoxy of the Church, was allowed, and those who would have given some teaching of love and hope based on inner or esoteric knowledge had to go into hiding for fear of persecution. Many individuals, and such groups as the Gnostics, the Essenes and a small brave sect in France called the Albigenses (destroyed for their beliefs), were all instrumental through their courage and silence in passing on the essentials of the wisdom teaching.

Thus valuable esoteric knowledge was constantly being developed and preserved by the underground philosophers of that time. The Neo-Platonists with their wealth of Pythagorean lore; the alchemists and astrologers who, until the light of the Renaissance had fully broken in upon the darkened world, used cyphers, symbols, cryptograms and alchemical formulae to protect the truths that no one dared to express openly.

As mirth is never completely extinguishable, even in despair, no doubt some of these spiritual stalwarts chuckled occasionally at having thus been able to conceal precious fragments of truth from the persecuting orthodoxy; for indeed, such phrases as the "philosopher's stone", the "elixir of life" and the "transmutation of base metal into gold", all of them relating to the regeneration of human nature, must have appeared as the ravings of lunatics or the babbling of fools to the average mentality.

To alleviate the mediaeval gloom and frustration, and under cover of their Christian flavour, inspiring stories of the Holy Grail and romantic tales of the Knights of King Arthur's Round Table spread through Europe, carried by wandering troubadours and jongleurs who sang, acted and mimed; often conveying inspiring messages, though usually no doubt in the crude forms of the time.

A mystical sense thus aroused was taken up by the Knights Templar—originally a military body whose founder during the Crusades had come into touch with eastern esoteric teachings through Arabian contacts. From this source came knowledge of the Jewish mystical Kabbalah as well as the mysterious Tarot cards—the origin of our own modern playing cards. Later, these knights came under the spell of materialism, but meanwhile they certainly added their quota to the spiritual life-line of esoteric teaching, then only shimmering precariously in the darkness.

During the fourteenth century a few of the brave savants in hiding gathered round a mysterious figure from Thuringia in Germany who had appeared under the symbolic name of Christian Rosencreutz. This group was important as they revived certain ancient teachings under the name Rosicrucian, and took for their chief emblem the symbol of the Rose and the Cross. This, with another of their symbols, the pelican feeding her young with blood from her own heart (both denoting supreme sacrifice), are still used by descendants of the original body of Rosicrucians, whoever they may have been. Some writers on Freemasonry have acknowledged either its descent from or the existence of some relationship with Rosicrucianism which has come down to modern times from the Ancient Mysteries.

There is another exalted piece of symbolism attributed to Christian Rosencreutz, namely the "House of the Holy Spirit", which gives rise to inspiring thoughts. It is a symbol which can be well understood today through the science of telepathy, especially in its deeper and more inclusive sense as "the science of impression" as it is described by "The Tibetan" in a book named *Telepathy and the Etheric Vehicle*,* wherein its function and importance are stressed. The deep significance to esoteric teaching of this symbolic "House of the Holy Spirit" cannot be overestimated. It was indeed "a house not made with hands", but denoted a state of lofty meditation within which these brethren had agreed to meet at stated times. Could this be a reflection of certain conclaves of the Great White Brotherhood itself? On this subject the following paragraphs may throw some light.

---

*Alice A. Bailey.

5.   *The Great Decision*

The Ageless Wisdom tells of regularly occurring cyclic conclaves of the Great White Brotherhood resulting in the stimulation and definite advance of esoteric thought and teaching
experienced during the last quarter of every century, and
also of similar encouragement and plans laid during the first
quarter.

There are many who will remember that an intensification
of interest in occult matters did indeed occur during the first
quarter of this present century. The teachings of Theosophy,
The Theosophical Society itself, Krishnamurti's revolutionary
approach to life and the first printing (in 1922) of the earlier
writings of "The Tibetan" (written down at dictation by Alice A.
Bailey) all either received fresh impetus as in the first two cases
or appeared for the first time as in the case of the latter. The
result was a general awakening, which has continued through
the years. This is clarified in a later section.

The source, cause and meaning of these periodical stimu-
lations are of vital interest to all esotericists. Important information is given on this subject in *A Treatise on White Magic*, p. 402,
by "The Tibetan". It seems that during the darkest phase of
world history since the worst days of Atlantis, a decision of
supreme importance was arrived at by the inner Council of the
Hierarchy who, owing to a temporary ascendence of the powers
of darkness, had deliberately withdrawn from the close contact
with humanity that had existed in Atlantean times. Towards the
end of the fourteenth century, during an epoch-making conclave, a far-reaching decision was taken to begin to establish
once again a close relationship with mankind. This was intended to foster the recurring centennial stimulation and to continue through the centuries onward into the now approaching Age
of Aquarius.

This tremendous plan, which was part of the Great Plan
put into operation, was destined to develop gradually and to
prepare the way for that coming event described as "The
Externalisation of the Hierarchy" by "The Tibetan" in a volume
of that title. This would be a foreshadowing of the time when
once again the "gods will walk with man" as of yore, but with a
difference, as even at the beginning of such externalisation at
least a portion of humanity will be working consciously as co-

operators with the Elder Brethren. This is seen as a training and a preparation for the greatest of all events, one which many all over the world await and describe in quite different terminologies; namely the reappearance of the Christ, or the Lord Maitreya, the Imam Mahdi, the Messiah—different names for the same great being who once said clearly "other sheep have I, who are not of this fold".

CHAPTER THREE

THE EMERGING PATTERN

1. *The Renaissance*

The first observable effect of the Great Decision was the emergence and flowering of culture during the Renaissance which spread all over Europe. The following excerpts from the chapter entitled "Rosicrucian and Masonic Origins" in *Lectures on Ancient Philosophy* by Manly P. Hall are enlightening regarding the spiritual awakening that followed the Dark Ages:

"The Mysteries of Egypt and Persia that had found a haven in the Arabian Desert reached Europe by way of the Knights Templar and Rosicrucians. . . . From far places of Irak and the hidden retreats of the Sufi Mystics the Ancient Wisdom found its way to Europe. A philosophic Clan, as it were, moved across the face of Europe under such names as 'The Illuminati' and the Rosicrucians. . . . One of the truly great minds of the secret fraternity—in fact the moving spirit of the whole enterprise—was Sir Francis Bacon."

The importance to esoteric as well as to outer knowledge of this great soul, Sir Francis Bacon, has been stressed in many occult writings in the west; these have suggested his being known in other incarnations as Roger Bacon (earlier than Francis), Hunyadi Janos, Christian Rosencreutz and Prince Rakoczi of Hungary, who was later known as the Comte de St Germain during the time of the French Revolution. Many today allude to him as the Master, the Prince.

After the Renaissance came the Reformation, followed in later centuries by the French Revolution and the Industrial Revolution in England. Outwardly each of these great advances or upheavals stood for a different kind of release and progress, each producing its own needed type of great souls or revolutionary leaders. From an esoteric viewpoint each stimulation resulted in a gradual bringing together of units into small groups and these into larger ones through common cause or similar interest. In this manner there developed a slow movement towards an eventual synthesis which, although only very partially achieved today, was part of the basic intent inherent in the Great Decision taken at the end of the fourteenth century.

During the sixteenth century and onwards such musicians as Tallis and Byrd in England, and their contemporaries in other parts of Europe, were awakening the soul to the ennobling influence of fine music in preparation for such sublime grandeur as that of Bach and Beethoven. Those whom we today call the Old Masters had already been educating the eye to the subtleties of colour and line and to the mental stimulation of proportion and perspective, while drama and mime vivified the imagination, and poetry, expressing mystical experience, was arousing an intuitive perception and the appreciation of beauty both seen and unseen.

Mainly behind the scenes, and contributing to the inner development of both mind and soul, were the "Illuminati" creating new forms and methods for imparting esoteric truths. These men were the later alchemists and Rosicrucians and also the Kabbalists who demonstrated the age-old teaching of man's nature and that of the universe in a symbolic glyph called the Tree of Life (one of several such "trees"). Although no longer in hiding, these later philosophic writers often preserved a degree of anonymity concerning some of their work, as indeed did Francis Bacon himself.

Through the introduction of printing and the consequent revival and spread of ancient learning and classical knowledge, a rebirth of thought and art in many countries had succeeded in rousing the world from the apathy of the Middle Ages, and as a result of the Reformation the long reign of the Pope had ended. From this release, in which some thought that "the baby was thrown out with the bath water" (as the mystical influence of the Roman Church was withdrawn), a revival of one of the most fundamental of the Ancient Mystery teachings began to spread. This was the fact that the earth was neither flat nor was it the supreme centre of the universe, but, as earlier pronounced by the ancient Greek astronomers, Hipparchus and Aristarchus, it was circular and revolved around the sun, which was the central orb.

The effect of this recovered knowledge on all contemporary life and thought was profound when brought to light through Galileo, who was later forced by the Inquisition to retract his statements, and also through Copernicus whose book *On The Revolution of Heavenly Bodies* was, fortunately for him, not published till after his death in 1543.

This entire revolution in human thinking opened the way for the necessary entry of the age of materialistic science, the forerunner of the science of today which, after the amazing atomic discoveries of this century, is now exploring the first of the non-physical fields, namely the etheric region, and in so doing is beginning to close the gap in thought between exoteric and esoteric science.

Thus did the burst of illumination of the Renaissance, carried on through successive centuries, vivify the golden life-line of spiritual continuity, carrying it through a long period of materialistic conservatism and bringing it eventually to the threshold of our own times.

2.   *Nineteenth Century—Stirring*

The appearance of H. P. Blavatsky's *The Secret Doctrine* during the last quarter of the nineteenth century caused a deep and uncomfortable stirring for many thoughtful people. It came as a shock to the intelligentsia, who at first met it with incredulity and ridicule which slowly gave way to interest. However, among occult students and those truly interested in esoteric subjects recognition of the vital importance of this work to both present and future generations placed it in a special category of its own.

The publication of this outstanding book was soon followed by the foundation of The Theosophical Society, sponsored, it is thought, by two members of the Great White Brotherhood: the Master Morya and the Master Koot Hoomi. It was these two great teachers, aided by one of their chief disciples—now known as the Master Djwhal Khul, The Tibetan—who had inspired and helped Madame Blavatsky to produce *The Secret Doctrine*, which deals with such tremendous issues as the creation and the innermost structure and nature of every thing from Cosmos to atom. Truly a masterpiece!

Developing at the same time as The Theosophical Society and the theosophical teachings, which have spread far beyond the borders of the organisation, were the Christian Science school of thought, the Spiritualist movement and also the New Thought movement which, as the name implies, sought in its diverse groups to acquaint people with the nature of thought and to train them in the right use of this little-understood power. At the same time astrology was beginning to be studied seriously by a small number of students, who were laying the foundation for the time when this age-old science could once more be used in conjunction with psychology, education and medicine and would enter the cosmic field where it truly belongs, as has been shown in a book by The Tibetan that revolutionises ordinary thinking on this vast subject.*

As a necessary and restraining influence to balance the increasing interest in all forms of psychism and its phenomena and to provide security against deception and credulity, a few well-known scientists such as Crookes, Myers and Oliver Lodge instituted the beginnings of the Society for Psychical Research, which aimed at investigation into such phenomena in a scientific manner.

Further evidence for the continuity of esoteric teaching was the reappearance in modern terms of the Rosicrucian tenets in such works as those of Max Heindel and other writers. Rudolph Steiner—once a leader within The Theosophical Society—formed his own group which, like the Rosicrucians, emphasised the Christian tradition, whereas the theosophic schools of thought accentuated the eastern approach. A meeting of east and west in philosophic and psychological thinking could be seen in the introduction of the teachings and practice of Yoga in forms adapted to western need and capacity. Sufi-ism, a mystical interpretation of the Islamic creed, was also becoming known to the mystically inclined of the western world.

These many different approaches to the Ageless Wisdom, all arising from the same basic origins, embodying the same eternal truths and inspired (according to their usefulness) by the Hierarchy, are still here today. They will meet the new age challenge inherent in the nature of the zodiacal sign of Aquarius, which demands change in every department of human thought and life. For the "ruling" planet of Aquarius is Uranus, most accurately designated the Awakener.

3. *Twentieth Century—Awakening*

To the truth-seeker of today the most encouraging sign as we come near to the last twenty-five years of our century is the

---

Esoteric Astrology, Vol. III of *A Treatise on The Seven Rays*, by Alice A. Bailey.

present intensification of the golden life-line of esoteric thought. Especially is this evident in the deepening and open-minded interest in the various branches of the Ageless Wisdom. We may now become aware of Hierarchical attention to world affairs as once again the approach of the end-of-century stimulation at all levels of experience may be felt. This energising influence naturally affects the evil as well as the good; for power in itself is neither of these but can be appropriated by either. Herein is man's opportunity to learn discernment, right choice (for him) and, within karmic limits, a measure of free will. To consider the undoubted upheavals of our time as an awakening due to this inflow of power is esoterically educational if seen within the larger evolutionary picture.

Important among those societies and groups existing at the turn of the last century was the Co-Masonic Order, which accepts both men and women. Its basic intent, especially in those countries where Theosophy was strongly grounded, was to elucidate and to stress the deep esoteric teaching which the rituals, allegories and symbols of Freemasonry are intended to convey, seeing the entire Fraternity as a reflection and continuation of the Ancient Mysteries and as an augur for their later return in forms far more suitable to Aquarian need and outlook.

Older students will remember that during the first quarter of this century there was a strong wave of intensified interest in the Ancient Wisdom felt round about the year 1925 and onwards. At this time certain revealing shocks were experienced, painful to all but the progressively minded and those who realised that, however respected and loved the teacher might be, it was always the TEACHING that was of prime consequence. An indication of some of the conditions then prevailing may prove instructive as a key to present and future trends.

At that time a strong challenge to orthodoxy in esoteric thinking had made its appearance, to which three main factors of differing qualities and strength seem to have been the main contributors:

1. Interpretations of the Secret Doctrine by very well qualified students such as Mrs Besant and her pupils were met with stern disapproval and even censure by what was termed a "Back to Blavatsky" movement.

2. About this time Krishnamurti dissolved the organisation known as The Order of the Star, founded for his use by theosophic leaders, and took an entirely different line from the one expected. His drastic treatment of all traditional habits of thinking, concerning national, personal and esoteric matters, proved shattering to very many of his followers, some of whom are today most grateful for that rousing experience.

3. In 1922 the first of The Tibetan's volumes of new age teaching were published. These works were either ignored or rejected by many for whom they were at first intended. Nevertheless, they have proved to be the foundation works on esoteric thought for this new age for a very large and world-wide students' group and for an increasingly extensive reading public at intelligentsia level. Repercussions of this rejection have been far-reaching and unfortunately retarding.

From the foregoing it may be gathered that reliance on authority had created a situation which, natural though it was to the Piscean outlook of the time, needed to be dissolved and reformed into a pattern of thought capable of adaptation to the new era which was even then recognised as approaching.

Looking to the future, one may reasonably expect that a crystallisation of what is now new age will once again become a danger to the minds of our successors—who could well be ourselves in future incarnations.

4.   *Twenty-first Century—Vision*

At the great Conclave of the Hierarchy held about the year 1400, when the decision was taken to approach nearer to humanity again, the plans for each end-of-century stimulation were laid. The overall objective was to combat the selfish and separative tendencies in man by working towards a then distant synthesis through the fostering and progressive growth of group work. The Hierarchy had in view the gradual development by degrees of a world religion and the restoration of the Mysteries in a new age form. Such beginnings would be preparatory to that greatest of all events, expressed today in different terms as the reappearance of the Christ. Such ideas have been forming, changing and reshaping in past decades, as students of the Ageless Wisdom will doubtless remember.

We read on page 406 of *A Treatise on White Magic* that within what was called a new world order there were to be seven main groups, and that the first four were "the cultural, the political, the religious and the scientific; in that order". These were to be followed by three more, namely "the philosophical, the psychological and lastly the financial or economic group". Today we can see how closely the pattern has worked out in just this order, even down to the last, the financial or economic group which today is working for improvement in the standards of human living, although for a while to come motives are likely to be mixed.

The most important group of all is a subjective one, the "hope for the new age" as that worldwide body known as "The New Group of World Servers" has been called. It has no outer plane organisation, and those who belong to it are often totally unaware of their inclusion in any such category. They are of any class, of any nationality, of any creed or of none. World betterment and human well-being at all levels mean more to them than their own individual or parochial concerns, though responsibility for these are not neglected.

Among this group of world servers are aspirants, probationary disciples, disciples and initiates of the earlier degrees. Some of these are working out in the world, a few being in key positions with no idea of their inner status, while many are working quietly from behind the scenes. The outstanding among them can be recognised for their moral courage, wisdom, breadth of view and an impersonality that has never lost the human touch; but perhaps above all for their capacity to "keep on keeping on", which a well-tried and tested disciple once told a wondering friend was the secret of her work. This ever increasing group forms a link in the world between the Hierarchy and humanity, a vital channel of communication whereby the former can contact the latter.

Three discoveries, all imminent and important, are described in *A Treatise on White Magic*, p. 333 (published 1934). The first concerns the release of power within the atom, already a subject of experiment at that time. The second deals with investigations regarding light and colour, producing another type of discovery, namely etheric vision, which today is by no means unusual. The third arises from the study of sound and "will put into man's hands a tremendous instrument in the world of creation. . . . The release of energy in the atom is linked to this new coming science of sound." To these three discoveries must be added another mentioned by The Tibetan in *A Treatise on Cosmic Fire*,* p. 675 (published 1925), namely the discovery of a third type of electricity, which will "put man in touch with extra-systemic phenomena".

A degree of space conquest and the possibility of inter-planetary communication are with us today. We already have light, colour and even the beginning of sound therapy. In con-nection with sound in its form of music and the human voice, we are informed from the same source[†] that new knowledge of correct breathing will produce a refinement and power within the voice which, when accompanied by lofty and concentrated thought, will have an effect we can at present hardly imagine. To some extent no doubt such a type of controlled thinking accom-panying a musical performance can even today enhance and elevate it according to the capacity of both performers and audi-ence so to think.

Various degrees of spiritual and psychic healing are already with us, while telepathy, in its larger aspect of "the science of impression", radiesthesia and E.S.P. of several kinds are on the way to proving the inter-relation of the different ranges of the one universal energy, or to express it otherwise, the interpene-tration of all the seven planes of our solar system.

War, with its aftermath of misery for millions, has shaken humanity into new approaches to life and has driven the eso-teric student into new dimensions of inquiry. Thoughtful man is now able to contemplate that vision of wholeness through which he can realise the possibility of a universe composed of states other than the physical, in which he as an individual can think of himself as an integral and similarly constituted minute whole. Esoteric science makes these ideas understandable, and since the release of atomic energy they are being tentatively approached step by step by the new age scientist as he probes further afield in his researches.

The tremendous changes during even the past ten years in human thinking have encouraged a widespread interest in such

---

*Alice A. Bailey.
[†]*Glamour: A World Problem* by Alice A. Bailey, p. 259.

ideas as those of reincarnation and the law of cause and effect, or Karma. Through even a little understanding of their joint operation, the logic of the existence of those "Just men made perfect", the Great White Brotherhood, is apparent. As the custodians and guides of the Plan for our earth, their projects are drawn up for centuries and even millennia ahead. The Plan, which is in reality God's purpose in action, becomes discernible through its own emerging patterns, some of which we have followed in this outline. Purpose cannot be frustrated, but the Plan can be, and it is sometimes delayed by the need for human free will to develop through experience towards divine will or purpose. "Not my will, but thine be done" is no mere pious utterance, but the cry of the last great World Teacher who went through all experience to demonstrate to mankind the GREAT LAW behind these words.

CHAPTER FOUR

TRANSITION

1. *From Pisces to Aquarius*

One of the most important of the Ageless Wisdom teachings, essential to some understanding of our own times, is based on the Law of Periodicity, or time cycles, and concerns the slow transition of the sun (from the earth's standpoint) from one sign of the zodiac into the next. This periodic change, which occurs every two thousand one hundred and sixty years and which is now taking place, is an astronomical event related to the precession of the equinoxes, the inner meaning of which may be learnt through some study of astrology. Even a little knowledge of this ancient science throws light on these cyclic changes, including the present one, as we experience the passing of the Age of Pisces and our entry into the approaching Age of Aquarius.

From the standpoint of astrology each of the twelve signs of the zodiac is considered as having a special affinity with one of the four elements of earth, water, fire or air. At present the sun is passing away from the influence of the sign of Pisces, the Fishes, related to the element of water which is the occult symbol for the emotional level of life. It was during the Piscean era that great advance was made in the control of the watery element through the use of its harnessed energy and also in the considerable control made by humanity over the emotions, symbolised in the New Testament by Christ's walking on the water and his calming of the waves. Emotion raised to its highest level, namely compassion, is the very essence of the new commandment given at the beginning of the Piscean era and the greatest works of the mystics, artists, musicians, poets and philosophers of this passing era have all contributed towards the upliftment of emotion into its higher complement of compassion. This is of course only partially achieved as yet, for in a universe of continuous creation wherein achievements and beginnings are but relative they must necessarily overlap within the realm of time.

Today an increasing mastery of the air is evident as we approach the air-minded sign of Aquarius known as "The Water

27

Bearer—Bearer of the Waters of Knowledge". This is typified pictorially by a man dispensing such gifts from his pitcher so that humanity, through a new quality of understanding (one of the basic Aquarian qualities), can realise something of the nature and the inter-relationship of the universe, Deity and man. This was recently made possible to the scientific inquirer by the break-through of science into the etheric region, and the consequent opening up of esoteric science for those who need this now proven etheric bridge from the dense physical level into the next realm called the astral, and then to the mental level and beyond.

Each sign of the zodiac has, in astrological language, its own planetary ruler, a planet especially in harmony with its own nature. Uranus, drastic and often shattering in its effects, and known as the awakener and liberator, is the ruler of Aquarius. However, Saturn, by reason of the delays and obstructions his influence can cause, is considered as sharing this rulership during the earlier phases of the Aquarian dispensation, and events of our time would indeed seem to confirm this idea of shared rulership. Drastic Uranian effects have already been experienced in the two world wars: in the splitting of the atom and, most markedly, in the breaking up of old habits of thinking, or "thoughtforms", thus clearing the decks for the building of a new outlook and the constructive use of released energy already being planned by the foremost thinkers of today.

This transition from one age to another is a repetition of former transitions which differ considerably from each other. For every successive cyclic change takes place at a higher level of the spiral of evolution, bringing in the next phase of world development, the last one having begun with our entry into the Christian era. At the start of a new cycle it may be difficult to see any distinctive advance which is inherent in the unfamiliar quality of the new zodiacal sign entangled for a while in old customs and habits. It was this condition that earlier produced a heartfelt cry from the great Indian poet Tagore, as he exclaimed, "Out of the dreary desert sand of dead habit, let my country awake!"* And today, the whole world is engaged in that very awakening.

This increase of man's power to respond to mental stimulus, which really means his growing capacity to think for himself,

---

*From "Sadhana" by Tagore.

is encouraging when we remember that the keynotes of the incoming Aquarian influence are not only understanding, but also service and sharing (from that symbolical pitcher). At first the response appears in the form of a predominating *self*-interest, which, through pressure of circumstances, is almost forced into what has been called "*enlightened* self-interest". For it is only through actually experiencing our interdependence as individuals, groups, nations and races (and also planets) that a new design for thinking, and therefore for living, begins to take shape.

Guiding the fresh energies as they enter our world and begin to form the new dispensation stands the Hierarchy, strengthening desirable trends and eliminating others to the extent to which the development of free will in humanity makes this possible. This is an important point to remember as we enter the last quarter of the twentieth century, which brings with it a special inflow of power from these true guides of our planet. This stimulation accompanies the incoming Aquarian influence and is a double event of extreme importance not experienced for two thousand years. And that is by no means all. In the Ageless Wisdom teaching of today there is much new instruction given about the outgoing Sixth Ray of Devotion which is now giving place to the Seventh Ray of Ceremonial Order—as it is called; the former being related to Pisces in quality and the latter (the Seventh Ray) to Aquarius. This tremendous subject of the seven great rays of manifestation and their cyclic waxing and waning in power, their collective representation of an entirely new spiritual psychology affecting all levels of living, is an integral part of the new age esoteric science; and although it seems relevant to mention it here, more cannot be said at this point.

It was at the Last Supper, that great symbolical feast which took place during the previous transition period, when the sun was passing from Aries the Ram to Pisces the Fishes, that Christ looking far ahead into what was then the future told the disciples in a cryptic utterance to go into the city, and that there they would meet the man with a pitcher of water; they were told to follow him. It would seem that thereby a strong sense of continuity was established, and a prophecy recorded for a then distant posterity although the tremendous experience of the whole of the Piscean era was still before the world.

2.   *Esoteric Groups in the Transition Period*

In *Letters on Occult Meditation* by The Tibetan (published 1922) certain descriptions of a prophetic nature were made concerning the first new age schools and groups. It was shown that an entirely Aquarian esoteric school would not be possible until the next century and that smallness in numbers and a definitely preparatory quality would characterise the first attempts. The work of these earlier groups would, to begin with, be mainly concerned with helping the student to find out for himself through his own study and self-imposed discipline. For only at the end of this century or at the beginning of the next will a few teachers having the requisite occult standing and insight begin to give the necessary training for Initiation in schools that then only will have become truly new age in character.*

The Aquarian seeker of today, although intensely independent in thought, is group-conscious, uninhibited and easily mixes with other inquirers. He is fearlessly attracted by all that can enlarge his outlook, whether it be through esoteric science or the latest findings of material science, through the study of comparative religion or within the varied fields of culture. He shows a keen interest in world affairs, each aspect of which he finds illumined through his esoteric study, even in the early stages. It is of little importance under which "ism" a man may search, if indeed under any, for the new age mentality is quick to discover the synthesis underlying the different approaches and will use any appropriate terminology without becoming bound by it or caught up in the use of trite slogans.

The above is a broad generalisation. We shall, however, appreciate the deeper Aquarian nature and thereby enter into the spirit of the newer teaching by noting the characteristics of those few who are today seriously attracted to the small and new esoteric groups. Their task is to introduce the next phase of esoteric teaching on a higher level in a more mental and therefore less emotional approach than hitherto; laying stress on the importance of the teaching rather than the teacher—no matter in how high an esteem the latter may be held.

The new age aspirant—and to a greater degree the disciple and even more so the initiate—is humane in outlook and non-

---

*See *Letters on Occult Meditation*. Letter IX.

possessive in human relationships. He is large-hearted and inclusive as well as being impersonal and quite unsentimental in his approach to reality, and just because he is not englamoured by sentimentality he can be truly compassionate. These qualities will be expressed through a well developed and balanced personality and an actively creative mind more interested in ideas than in personalities. He will be capable of enough abstract thought to understand and think in terms of wholeness and will work for the larger whole, to which end he may often have to sacrifice individual feelings—certainly in himself and sometimes in others. Naturally enough such people are often considered cold and "unspiritual" by those who are deeply Piscean in outlook. A word of warning however is timely here, for the fault of the early and as yet unmellowed Aquarian is indeed ruthlessness. And occasions will arise when he and even his more developed brother could appear unsympathetic to many of their companions.

We should realise that today many of the long established esoteric schools, whether known to themselves or not, or even in some cases in spite of themselves, are already moving with the progressive urge now sweeping the entire world and which in a subtler and deeper sense permeates the new esoteric teaching for today and for many of our tomorrows. We might recall some of the better known groups and organisations now working in the west on various lines. There are the many and differing schools of Yoga throughout the east and some now in the west; Theosophy, Rosicrucianism, the school of Ouspensky, The Philosophical Research Society in California founded by Manly P. Hall, as well as others in America; the schools of Rudolph Steiner, astrological groups, spiritualistic churches and centres, and many E.S.P. and psychic research organisations and their offshoots. The foundational work contained in *The Secret Doctrine* of H. P. Blavatsky has been further expounded, together with much new teaching revealed explicitly for this coming new era by The Tibetan Teacher, through Alice A. Bailey. The Arcane School is based on this teaching and its meaning for the new age.

It is likely that many esoteric students and seekers of today will find the following quotation from *The Rays and the Initiations* (Vol. V of *A Treatise on the Seven Rays*) of considerable interest. This book of 750 pages is the last of the sequence of nineteen volumes of new age esoteric teaching dictated by mental telepathy over a period of thirty years from 1919 to 1949 through Alice A. Bailey (in her waking consciousness) by The Tibetan, the Master Djwhal Khul.* These following short paragraphs indicate teaching for an entire century containing a further period of instruction called "revelatory" to emerge after 1975: they give a condensed and vivid picture of where we stand today with regard to these periodically appearing new chapters of that endless book we call the Ancient or the Ageless Wisdom.

". . . the teaching which I have given out has been intermediate in nature, just as that given by H. P. B. under my instruction has been preparatory. The teaching planned by the Hierarchy to precede and condition the New Age, falls into three categories:

"1. Preparatory, given 1875–1890 . . . written down by H. P. B.

"2. Intermediate, given 1919–1949 . . . written down by A. A. B.

"3. Revelatory, emerging after 1975 . . . to be given on a world wide scale via the radio.

"In the next century, and early in the century, an initiate will appear and will carry on this teaching. It will be under the same 'impression', for my task is not yet completed, and this series of bridging treatises between the material knowledge of man and the science of the initiates has still another phase to run. The remainder of this century, as I told you elsewhere (*Destiny of the Nations*, p. 106), must be dedicated to rebuilding the shrine of man's living, to reconstructing the form of humanity's life, to reconstituting the new civilisation upon the foundations of the old, and to the reorganising of the structures of world thought, world politics, plus the redistribution of the world's resources in conformity to divine purpose. Then, and only then will it be possible to carry the revelation further." (*The Rays and the Initiations*, p. 255.)

---

*In addition, there are five books which Mrs. Bailey wrote herself, including *The Unfinished Autobiography*.

3. *Esoteric Teaching for The New Age*

There exists today a wealth of teaching which has arisen in answer to the need for esoteric truth to be expressed in keeping with the mental outlook and in the language of our time.

Further revelation was presented and a consequent reorientation of thought has been taking place. However, it is advisable to hold an unfamiliar idea or a deeper interpretation as a reasonable hypothesis until the ring of its inherent truth awakens intuition or until plain logic indicates that it makes sense with that which is already known and understood.

Only the very barest indication of some of the aspects of the new age teaching is possible, and the reader is referred to suggestions for reading at the end of this book.

(a) *The "Energy" Concept*

Underlying the new age esoteric instructions, and elucidating the meaning of those ancient maxims "As above, so below" and "Man is made in the image of God", is the following all-important statement, namely that "ALL IS ENERGY".

In the light of this illuminating sentence the age-old concept of wholeness becomes vital and more significant. For this saying is the modern version of the statement made by H. P. Blavatsky in *The Secret Doctrine* that densest matter is spirit at its lowest level, while spirit is matter raised through infinite gradations to its highest. The idea that "All is Energy", which is held by many advanced scientists today, opens the way for the linking up of esoteric and material science. Material science has already penetrated into the next finer grade of existence, namely the etheric. Is it perhaps conceivable that in the future the two sciences will meet at a considerably higher level than that of the etheric, and will form one science, the science of life? Could this be the point at which material science will discover for itself the existence of the soul as already predicted in the following words?

"The next step ahead for science is the discovery of the soul, a discovery which will revolutionise, though not negate, the majority of their theories."*

Esoteric Healing by Alice A. Bailey. Vol. IV: *A Treatise on The Seven Rays.*

(b)　*The Hierarchy and the Great Plan*

Together with much new information we find a virile and realistic approach to the Hierarchy, the Inner Government of our world which while it inspires also demonstrates the practical nature and the logical necessity of the existence of the body of "Just men made perfect".

This is an alive presentation of the Hierarchy, beginning with the initiated disciple of lowest degree, a number of whom are in incarnation. From there we are taken up through the grades of senior initiates to the Masters of Wisdom; through the still higher levels of the Christ and the Buddha within the great Council of Shamballa; and again beyond to the great Beings who connect our planet with other planets of the solar system and those whose incomprehensible task it is to be the links with sources of power beyond this system.

Here we have an unbroken chain, or energy channel, which at its lowest level on the physical plane makes contact with the many aspirants and disciples within the widely spread Group of World Servers, who either consciously or unconsciously act according to hierarchical influence to the best of their ability. Considered in terms of energy, we can perceive the underlying synthesis and unity of a great whole.

The Masters are the custodians and also the executors for our planet of the Great Plan, which consists of three main departments: (1) Government and Races, (2) Religion, in its wider senses, (3) Civilisation and culture, and the subdivisions of these. All this engrosses their attention as well as work with the sub-human kingdoms and with the angelic or deva kingdom.

We are all involved in the Plan to the extent to which a group, a nation, or an individual becomes of relative importance to some portion of it, and is sensitive to the reception of instruction for the work. This takes the form of what is called "impression" (mental telepathy), which filters through to the brain as an idea, an ideal or simply a hunch. The recipient usually has no realisation of its origin and proceeds to work with it as if it were his own. The form in which he has registered it may or may not contain distortions.

(c) *The Seven Rays of Manifestation*

"The New Spiritual Psychology" is the description given to this all-embracing ray teaching. Everything from atom to the highest entity belongs to, is qualified by, or has a special affinity with, one or more of the Seven Great Rays of Manifestation. These permeate and condition all existence, *The Book of Revelation* refers to them as "The Seven Spirits before the Throne". The main characteristic of each ray is indicated by the following words:

Ray I. POWER; II. LOVE-WISDOM; III. DIVINE INTELLIGENCE. These first three rays are known as the major rays and correspond to the Trinity found in the great religions of the world.

Then come Ray IV. HARMONY (through conflict); V. MENTALITY; VI. DEVOTION and VII. RAY OF CEREMONIAL ORDER (or ORDERED ACTIVITY). All seven are equally important but one or two, sometimes three, are especially active during a given cycle. The seven rays correlate with the seven planes of the solar system and they qualify all the sevenfold divisions within every kingdom of nature. Ray II is always active, for this Ray of LOVE-WISDOM is the overall ray of our solar system.

From the angle of self-knowledge and of understanding the outlook and difficulties of other people and nations (since every nation is "on" a ray), this ray teaching is enlightening, giving a deep tolerance and an insight into motive.* The particular rays of monad, soul and personality are extensively dealt with, as well as the rays as applied to all the other kingdoms of nature. The need to know one's own soul ray is indicated, also the rays of the personality; i.e. of the mind, emotions and physical body which can all be on a different ray during one lifetime. It is not possible to know the monadic ray until an advanced stage; it never changes and is always on either Ray I, II or III. The soul ray may change, though it seldom does and during every successive life each of the three personality rays differs according to the karmic need of that life, as realised by the soul before incarnation.

To us, the cosmic aspect of this subject of the rays seems stupendous as it deals with planets, solar systems and mighty star consciousnesses, indicating great triangular relationships between them through ray affinity. This is within the fascinating

---

The Destiny of the Nations by Alice A. Bailey.

realm of esoteric astrology.* The astrologer with some grasp of astrological principles will gain a much wider vision as he reads even a little and reflects on this deeper approach to the science of astrology. It can then be seen how some knowledge of the seven rays throws light on the personal horoscope helping the individual to find his own field of work and indicating his lines of least resistance. Each sign of the zodiac and each planet is in special affinity with one, two and sometimes three of the rays.

(d) *The Ashram*

Everything in our world is a reflection of its own higher counterpart or prototype: "As above, so below"—and we might add as near as may be under the circumstances. It is in this sense that we can best understand the statement that the only real ashram exists at the Buddhic or intuitional level and that those so named on the physical plane are but very incomplete reflections of great prototypes.

There are seven great ashrams at this high level, each belonging to one of the seven rays with a Master of Wisdom of a particular ray at the head and with other masters, initiates and disciples of different grades either in or out of incarnation engaged in the work and the training in connection with their own particular ashram.

The word ashram has been used rather indiscriminately. It should denote only those serious groups who have gathered round a highly qualified teacher for truly spiritual instruction, and the consequent work that contributes towards the fulfilment of the Great Plan. For the true mystic of the new age cannot be a recluse in our times even though experience in his past incarnations tends to draw him in that direction. While looking first within, he then looks also without, thus relating the mystic insight with the occult outlook. It is said of him that "his ways will be unaccountable to many, but he will not offend. His words will never be trite or platitudinous and while clear and simple, they may cause a wonder, because the sense of them is a new sense to some, though nonsense to many."

This new sense is that of the new age of Aquarius, the next level of consciousness to that of the passing era—the sense which the real ashram inculcates and which motivates and inspires every new age seeker, aspirant and disciple.

Esoteric Astrology by Alice A. Bailey.

(e) *"The Antahkarana"—The Bridge*

The sutratma, or silver cord described in Ecclesiastes, which is withdrawn by stages into the soul at death, is familiar to the West. It is truly our individual continuity thread or life-line.

Knowledge of the antahkarana, or path of consciousness that will ultimately link physical plane man with his highest spiritual self, is new. All spiritual pioneers are bridging between the highest they already know and areas of awareness beyond. This bridge is built by the methods of the science of the antahkarana.

The construction of the antahkarana takes place almost automatically in the early stages. Humanity builds it first between the physical (etheric) and the astral or emotional level; then between that level and the concrete mind as the latter begins to control emotion, while today a minority among the more thoughtful are already beginning to form the bridge between the concrete and the abstract mind. This creation by man himself may be considered as the building of a channel or pathway in the inner worlds for that "new sense" already described.

There comes a time during some one life when the aspirant or the probationary disciple takes this matter deliberately in hand by a slow dispassionate application to the required study, a well regulated and balanced practice of meditation, and by carrying out the precepts of esoteric teaching in whatever walk of life he finds himself. The desired result is the gradual formation of a channel between the soul and personality and then later with the monadic or spiritual part of his being. First alignment—and eventually "at-one-ment". We have here the true meaning of "Atonement". Many people bring over from former lives a partially built channel of this description without being at all aware of the spiritual technique—to use a seemingly contradictory phrase. In the education of the future,* construction of the antahkarana will be included in the curriculum in the same way as today the building and maintaining of a healthy physical body is now being taught in school and college.

(f) *The Path of Discipleship*

Each new era demands and receives a further unveiling of hitherto esoteric instruction for the treading of the Path of Discipleship, or of "hastened evolution", as it is sometimes called.

---

*See *Education in the New Age* by Alice A. Bailey. Chapter V.

Today, although stress is laid on group training, and for the first time on group Initiation, the effort and the advancement are at the same time also distinctly individual.

Although requirements for treading the Path cannot at any time supersede the truly ancient and basic "rules of the road", they are framed anew, in a different setting and always at a higher level to meet the further understanding and extended vision of seekers in successive time cycles.

It is perhaps in connection with this subject of the Path more than any other that one is conscious of a new angle of approach and the continual disclosure of a new viewpoint. The new age presentation throughout is a constant divulgence of new modes of progressive thinking hinting at the existence of laws which at the time we are incapable of understanding.

The esoteric is continually becoming exoteric: that which we call new is all the time present. There is a constant unveiling of truth and what we are now beginning to put into practice as something new to us has long ago led others far ahead of where we stand today.

Many are today treading the steps of the Path of Discipleship,* passing from the stage called probationary to that of accepted discipleship and on to Initiation. In different areas of the world, and even within one city, various terms are used to describe this utterly real and inward journey of the soul.

The true Aquarian qualities and outlook give the key to the new approach to this great theme of the several stages on the Path of Discipleship leading to Initiation. All, even the most advanced on the Path, are disciples or learners. For the Masters of Wisdom themselves are evolving, and on reaching that level (at the fifth Initiation) the "Way of The Higher Evolution" begins to open out before them, giving the choice of the Seven Paths, only a few of which have any connection with humanity and our planet. In these days when men's minds are gradually opening out to the ideas of life on other planets contemplation on these lines contains the seeds of later knowledge for the human race.

---

*Discipleship in the New Age, Vols. I and II, by Alice A. Bailey.

CHAPTER FIVE

THE CHANGING FORM
OF THE MYSTERIES

1. *An Impact of Combined Energies*

An impact of exceptionally powerful influences affecting the world during our time can clearly be noted and somewhat understood through esoteric teachings, astronomy and astrology. Four of these influences have already been considered, but a short repetition of them together with two as yet unmentioned is required in order to emphasise the importance of their *combination*, especially in regard to the importance of the Mysteries—the continuity of which has been our theme.

The profound significance of this tremendous impact as it creates change at every level of existence underlies the whole of the last instalment of esoteric teaching given from the year 1919 to 1949 "planned by the Hierarchy to precede and condition the New Age". The several conditioning influences are:

1. The mingling of two different zodiacal qualities, the outgoing Piscean and the incoming Aquarian characteristics which together colour and energise this transition period as we enter a new 2,160 year cycle.

2. Coinciding with this lesser cycle we are also at the beginning of a greater one of 25,000 years' duration, as our sun, having completed a major revolution through the twelve signs of the zodiac, begins a new solar year which is also governed by the sign of Aquarius.

3. Simultaneously the influence of the sixth Ray of Devotion which is akin to Pisces in nature is now passing out as the incoming seventh Ray of Ceremonial Order (ordered activity)—having affinity with Aquarius—takes its place.

4. The widespread expectation of the reappearance of the Christ, expressed differently by the many religious, occult and mystical groups, as well as by individuals affiliated to none of these.

5. The unprecedented close grouping of seven planets in the sign of Aquarius at the time of the new moon of February 1962; an astronomical formation considered by some astrologers to mark the beginning of the earth's entry into the Age of Aquarius.

6. The approaching final quarter of the century stimulation from the Hierarchy; the last one in 1875 having been marked by the appearance of H. P. Blavatsky's *The Secret Doctrine* and the foundation of The Theosophical Society.

The concurrence and mingling of these potent forces make it impossible to estimate the outstanding importance of our time. It is not to be wondered at that the Hierarchy have described this particular period as the moment for which they have been preparing.

We may find it hard to realise that in spite of the world's unsettled and often chaotic conditions we are under an inner and beneficent direction of a deeply spiritual nature. Some people will see it as the guidance of the Hierarchy during the earth's most difficult decades: others, however, may call it the Love of God manifesting in very strange ways, for the effects of the new age influences on the minds of the unthinking are obviously disturbing. It is the esoteric teachings, even in their simplest statements, which give the assurance that we are indeed experiencing the preparation for a spiritual renaissance.

Looking below the seething surface of outer events we become aware of the spreading move towards the elimination of sectarian separativeness and an increasing distaste for reliance on hard and fast doctrine and dogma. At the same time there is an intensified search for a deeper understanding of the inner teachings and their application to the enormous problems of today.

2.   *The Three Main Channels for the Mysteries*

As stated earlier the overall theme of occult or esoteric teaching is WHOLENESS and the inter-relation and interdependence of its many parts. For the gradual revelation of truth to man in terms of WHAT he is and WHY he is, the Mysteries change their form of presentation from age to age, from century to century and in our time almost from decade to decade, so rapidly is the spiritual awakening of man taking place.

New and deeper aspects of the teachings are not only revealed through fresh information. Discernment of relationship between already known facts, the practice of reflective meditation, time allowed for wonder and the practical living of life in line with that which is already known in theory are all important factors towards further revelation and its understanding.

Descending from the Ancient Mystery schools and temples and in preparation for the new age there exist today three main channels for the Mysteries. These are Freemasonry, religion or the Church (by whatsoever name) and the Esoteric Group. This latter, which constitutes the innermost circle of all esoteric groups, is made up of all true spiritual esotericists found either within or outside the ranks of the many esoteric occult bodies.

At present these channels tend to conceal rather than to reveal the inner meaning within the form, but they nevertheless converge disclosing deeper aspects of truth as they approach their own inner sanctuaries.

"There is no dissociation between the One Universal Church, the sacred inner Lodge of all true Masons and the innermost circles of the esoteric societies. Three types of men have their need met, three major Rays are expressed and the three paths to the Master are trodden, leading all three to the same portal and the same Hierophant."*

When a new and universally oriented religion has sway and the nature of esotericism is better understood, the inwardly linked esoteric, masonic and church organisms will be used as centres for Initiation, which today is not the case. The first Initiation admits an individual to the outer precincts of the Hierarchy. A number of initiates of the first and some of the second degree are to be found within the Group of World Servers, that widely spread body forming the link between humanity and the Hierarchy. Such people are usually unaware of their inner status, being deeply engrossed in their work in the outer world. For the third Initiation (considered the First Great Initiation by the Hierarchy) a registration of its occurrence down here in the physical brain consciousness is entailed.

"These ancient Mysteries were originally given to humanity by the Hierarchy, and were—in their turn—received by the Hierarchy from the Great White Lodge on Sirius. They contain the clue to the evolutionary process, hidden in numbers and in words; they veil the secret of man's origin and destiny, picturing for him in rite and ritual the long, long path which he must tread. . . . I mention here the Masonic purpose because it is closely related to the restoration of the Mysteries

---

* *The Externalisation of the Hierarchy*, p. 513, by Alice A. Bailey.

and has held the clue—down the ages—to that long awaited Restoration. . . .*

"The ground is being prepared at this time for this great restoration. The Churches and Masonry are today before the judgment seat of humanity's critical mind and the word has gone forth . . . that both of them failed in their divinely assigned tasks."†

Approaching the three channels for the Mysteries from an esoteric standpoint, we may be led to some realisation of what each is *intended* to reveal, and thus find it possible to perceive the nature of desirable changes in form.

(a)   *Freemasonry*

This ritualistic descendant from the Ancient Mysteries emphasises the first of the three aspects of the Trinity, God the Father—power, rulership and kingship. It is therefore closely linked to the first Ray of Power, and particularly in this coming Aquarian Age to the seventh Ray of Ceremonial Order.

Among the many profound symbols of Freemasonry are the Temple and the Chair of King Solomon, that supreme and exceedingly wise earthly king, the representative (masonically speaking) of an infinitely higher and spiritual King. To the exalted position of ruler of his own Lodge, and representative of King Solomon, every Master Mason "in good standing" may in time aspire.

Among certain of the outstanding teachings of Freemasonry only a few can here be very briefly indicated:

1. A masonic lodge is esoterically seen as a miniature reflection of the universe, illustrating the ancient axiom "As above, so below". The basic duality of our solar system expressed as Love-Wisdom is preserved and illustrated symbolically in the two Great Pillars at the entrance to the Temple—which itself is one of the most wonderful of all the symbols: "Know ye not that *ye* are the Temple of The Most High?"

The inmost centre of our universe, Deity, is reflected in symbol in the centre of the lodge and is seen again as being mirrored within the heart of every individual. Numbers, especially

---

The Rays and The Initiations, p. 331.
†Ibid.

3, 5, 7 and 12, are among the numerical reflections of the Macrocosm into the microcosm (man).

2. As the lodge mirrors the universe, so does man reflect the lodge, the seven officers correlating with the sevenfold nature of his own being, beginning with the head, the "crown" centre or "chakra"* (in etheric matter): for this is the seat of will, purpose and direction. As rulership of the lodge means direction and its control by the Master through his seven officers, it illustrates and teaches the rulership and control to be gained by man over his own "lodge" or sevenfold being.

3. Freemasonry is a training ground for this very purpose and the allegories, rites, symbols and "penalties", cumbersome and outmoded though the *forms* of them are for the new age mentality, have been in past ages designed and preserved to this end. Through training and *spiritually merited* advancement through the degrees, significantly numbering 33, a man or woman is gradually raised towards the goal of "perfection", not only in this life, but during the course of successive incarnations.

By studying, understanding and by living according to what Freemasonry was primarily designed to teach, a mason can greatly hasten not only his own spiritual progress, but that of his many brethren also.

(b) *Religion*

This is the channel for the Mysteries as they assume that particular form known to us as religion. This word is derived from the Latin *religare* meaning to bind back, indicating how man may return to God through the attracting and binding influence of love in its very essence, and not only as an emotional and therefore an ephemeral experience—necessary stage though this may be.

Love-Wisdom is not only the basic quality of our solar system but also of the second ray, the chief ray for this system. This occult fact accounts for that best known of all biblical texts which affirms that God is Love. In its grand simplicity this is for us the most sublime truth as it constitutes the core of a great central Mystery. This, while still within the realms of esoteric

*See footnote on "chakras" on p. 49.

teaching, can, in its simpler form, be approached by the aspirant of open mind and understanding heart. Such an expression of it follows the next section, which deals with that third
channel for the Mysteries, namely the Esoteric Group.

There are other truths previously mentioned regarding
divine Love and Justice, among which are reincarnation, Karma
(cause and effect), teaching on man's invisible nature and his
relation through it to God and the universe: on death or "transition", on spiritual healing, on the Hierarchy and the existence
of the Great Plan: all of these if courageously investigated and
taught in simple language through the churches would bring
not only understanding but blessing to troubled minds, and fur-
thermore would generate a great dynamic incentive to true worship. However, there is increasing evidence among a few open-
minded clergy of the various denominations that these truths
are not unknown to them. The east has known and taught them
for many centuries.

God has so loved the world that he has sent not only one
but many Sons. Concerning the successive appearances of these
Beings a definite design is discernible, even within the limited
descriptions emerging from history which omit the inner significance, the sense of continuity and of relationship between
these periodic events. For example, it is not generally known
that Christ came to earth first as the earlier teacher Sri Krishna
before his incarnation as the founder of Christianity, and that
much later the Master Jesus overshadowed and inspired the
Prophet Mahomed during the latter's mission on earth. Again it
is new to the majority in the west that the Lord Buddha is in
touch with our world each year during the great Wesak festival
of the full moon of May, when he joins with Christ in a great out-
pouring of blessing on the world, and that he continually stands
behind his great Brother in preparation for Christ's own reappearance on earth. Here we have a close inner linking of four
great religions—Hindu, Buddhist, Christian and Moslem; part
of the great design of a tapestry interwoven with the Love of
God who sent these Sons (and earlier ones) to different peoples
of the earth, at the appointed time and with the appropriate
teaching for each.

Reconstruction is inevitably gradual, even today. In regard
to religious ideas, ideals and their expression in form it is still
compromise and a partial readjustment that must characterise

the transition period, while major obstacles dissolve under the increasing power of the new age energies as they are used by humanity itself to bring about the needed changes. When man has thus exerted himself to the best of his ability, and *only then*, is the Hierarchy empowered to take over and enable changes for the better to gain strength and momentum, and what appears to us as a miracle is accomplished.

Possibly we may observe such human efforts being assisted from behind the scenes during this and future decades in such events as the Second Vatican Ecumenical Council. This may well be the most significant conclave of written history. Will Pope Paul VI be able to continue and develop the revolutionary trends set in motion by his predecessor Pope John XXIII?

The World Council of Churches in conjunction with other Christians is having a strong influence in the general trend towards the beginnings of a convergence, though still within the distinct boundaries of one creed. It was perhaps Sir Francis Younghusband and his inclusive World Congress of Faiths, started many years ago, which gave the modern lead in this direction, together with those esoteric groups that have always stood for the basic unity lying behind all outward forms of religion.

Other fellowships of the various religions are now arising in different parts of the world. A great network of unity in diversity is being created as man comes nearer to realising the existent, eternal and underlying FACT of this unity. A continued expansion and deepening in this direction of this channel of the Mysteries can but strengthen and amplify the work of the other two, convergent as the three become on the way to the inmost sanctuary where they are truly ONE.

(c)   *The Esoteric Group*

Both Freemasonry and religion, or the Church of different creeds and denominations, possess deeply hidden within their own symbols and rites truths as yet unrealised or even imagined by the majority of their members, all of which lead towards a central Mystery. It is the Esoteric Group, the third channel for the Mysteries, more sensitive and open to the new energies impinging on the world, that will gradually permeate the other two bodies either directly or indirectly with fresh understanding and interpretation, which will help them to transform themselves into live organisms with the emphasis on their own in-dwelling life. It is just such an influx that will cause them to con-form to newly discovered depths of their own teachings, and therefore to *re*-form in outer presentation in keeping with new age need and widened outlook.

This fresh insight into the Will of God through a new sim-plicity, permeated with a new quality, must for a while remain closed to the majority; not because we arc still babes and must be guarded from knowing, but because such knowing depends upon the development of our own soul sense.

In conjunction with the purpose of this third channel for the Mysteries, the following quotation from *The Rays and The Initiations*, the last volume to be dictated by The Tibetan to Alice A. Bailey, is both prophetic and inspiring:

"The Mysteries will be restored in other ways also, for they contain much besides that which the Masonic rites can reveal or that religious rituals and ceremonies can disclose. . . . The Mysteries will restore colour and music as they essentially are to the world . . . in such a manner that the creative art of today will be to this new creative art what a child's building of wooden blocks is to a great cathedral such as Durham or Milan. The Mysteries, when restored, will make real—in a sense incompre-hensible to you at present—the nature of religion, the purpose of science and the goal of education. These are not what you think today . . ."*

We are told of a quality for which at present our language has no words. As the Aquarian Era advances humanity will begin to sense it. As the coming great Teacher will himself embody and teach it, it will perhaps become the key, the "new com-mandment" which during his last time with us was expressed in the injunction that we should "Love one another". Must we not at once admit that our achievement in this respect has been noticeably imperfect? However, in the overlapping of one time cycle with another, such as is the case today, the older com-mandment will receive fresh meaning for us in the light of that which is new. This new quality will in fact provide the seeker with that insight into his own nature which will illumine further the meaning of Love itself bringing us to the very threshold of the great central mystery of our own solar system.

The Rays and The Initiations, pp. 331–2.

3.   *A Central Mystery*

> "O Thou who givest sustenance to the universe
> From whom all things proceed
> To whom all things return,
> Unveil to us the face of the true Spiritual Sun
> Hidden by a disc of golden light
> That we may know the Truth
> And do our whole duty
> As we journey to Thy Sacred Feet."

Through this most sacred text of the ancient Vedas of India, "The Gayatri", the devout Brahman of today continues to greet the rising sun as have others before him during the passage of many thousands of years.

The central mystery embodied in the sun was a subject which filled the very ancient people with reverential awe. Later the element of fear and the need for the propitiation of a cruel deity developed in different parts of the world. It was the great and fearless King Akhnaton who re-established the idea among his own people, at least for a time, of the truly beneficent nature of the One Giver of Life to our earth.

Long before the reign of this benign king as well as afterwards some form of sun worship had existed, and each phase of esoteric teaching has given a grander conception and one nearer to the profound truth that lies behind it. The new age teachings given by The Tibetan further unfold this deep subject, especially in the two volumes *A Treatise on Cosmic Fire* and *Esoteric Astrology*. Herein the widespread network of relationship between our earth, the other planets, our sun and other solar systems, great star groups and the signs of the zodiac are shown as forming immense designs and smaller patterns of relationship: many of these being of intense interest to us as the world becomes aware of the possibility of interplanetary communication.

The greater scientists have acknowledged the existence of a Cosmic Intelligence at work in both designing and the regulation of the cosmos. They have also acknowledged the existence of an unbroken sequence of graded energies ranging from highest spirit to densest matter—the energy concept. Esoteric science has always recognised both these conceptions in the existence of a grand design consisting of smaller patterns based on number and reaching in unbroken continuity, as it were across the warp and woof of the loom of life. Upon and within this ever expanding and universal framework our imagination may picture the weaving of a patterned and beautiful brocade of many colours with their subtler shades as yet unperceived by us: the "spirit-stuff" of planets and their inhabitants, solar systems, galaxies and universes. Within this immensity dwells our own solar system, a tiny speck within the celestial folds of the Milky Way.

Regarding our present theme, namely the central mystery, the following illuminating quotation from *A Treatise on Cosmic Fire** followed by a table of its main statements is given:

"The Centre in the cosmic body of 'THE ONE ABOUT WHOM NAUGHT MAY BE SAID' of which our solar Logos is the embodied force is the *heart centre*. Here we have one of the clues to the mystery of electricity. The sacred planets (of our solar system) . . . are parts of that heart centre . . . of that great unknown Existence Who stands to our Solar Logos as he in his turn stands to the Heavenly Men who are His Centres. . . . Therefore it will be apparent to the careful student that the entire force and energy of the system and its life quality will be that which we call (having perforce to use handicapping and misleading words) LOVE. This will account for the fact that the force which plays through the cosmic heart centre will be the paramount force found in the manifestation of a solar Logos, and of a Heavenly Man; it will likewise produce its microcosmic analogy and reflective reactions; this force when rightly directed and properly controlled is the great transmuting agency which eventually will make of the human unit a Master of The Wisdom, a Lord of Love. . . ."

The implications of this transmission of the "Logoic Impulse" from its source through to the solar system, planets and humanity are vast and enlightening regarding the psychological problems of our day. The last inspiring sentence, indicating the truth that "when rightly directed this force is the great transmuting agency", gives one of the major revealing keys to esoteric teaching, always mystically acknowledged but seldom occultly understood.

**A Treatise on Cosmic Fire*, pp. 511–12.

Recalling that great Law of Correspondence and Analogy as illustrated by the saying "As above, so below", we might reflect on the following sequence of the main ideas from the above quotation:

1. The Being of that great Entity, referred to as "THE ONE ABOUT WHOM NAUGHT MAY BE SAID", is comprised of seven solar systems. One of these, our solar system, is the embodied force of the heart centre within this great entity.

2. Owing to his position as the heart centre within this Being, our Solar Logos transmits the heart quality which we call LOVE to all planets within the system.

3. Descending in scale to our own planet earth: the three chief centres in the life of our own Planetary Ruler or Logos are: Head Centre—Shamballa (will); Heart Centre—Hierarchy (love); and Throat Centre—Humanity (mentality). Herein it is the heart centre, the Hierarchy, which receives the great logoic impulse of Love and transmits it to earth.

4. Coming down in the scale still further to man, the individual, we see him as a tiny reflection of each of the above. He also has his seven centres or chakras* (as they are called in Indian Yogic philosophy). In our time it is the heart centre in man which is of supreme importance, for in the last analysis it is this heart quality of love which at its best leads man to the Highest.

---

*A note on the centres or "chakras".

In man who is a reflection in miniature of the Great Entity and of a solar system and also of a planet, the seven chief centres of etheric energies (whirling vortices of power when developed) are situated at intervals up the spinal column. These consist of two head centres, throat, heart, solar plexus, sacral and base of spine centres. Each one of these centres is connected with one of the endocrine glands of the dense physical body, making a vital connection between man's outer and his inner and invisible nature. As the seven etheric centres are both "inlets" as well as "outlets" for various levels of energy according to the stage of soul development and the individual's ray type, they can be seen to be of very great importance in health, physical, emotional and mental; and also of spiritual significance when channelling higher energies. These centres emanate radiatory discharges (varying tremendously in degrees of refinement or crudity) into the aura and thence into the environment in which one or many people may be congregated. In the completely unevolved, only the lower centres are as yet active. There is here a vast field for present and future physical, psychological and spiritual investigation.

At intervals throughout the new age teachings, The Tibetan draws our attention to the wonder of the unfolding Plan in such phrases as "See you not the beauty of the ordered scheme?". Especially is the mind so directed in connection with the many instances where the Law of Analogy or Correspondence discloses the graded sequence of patterned reflections from the great macrocosm of the universe down into the microcosm, man. For the use of the axiom "As above, so below" can reveal those truths which to us are indeed marvels, as the inside of a tiny acorn discloses the minute design of a future oak tree.

"The beauty of the ordered scheme" will become clearer to the mind's eye as the seventh Ray of Ceremonial Order (ordered activity) becomes increasingly potent. This ray influence together with others already described will be instrumental in setting in motion new rhythms of thought through which harmony will gradually supersede discord; and as humanity becomes more aware of the patterned structure of creation it will use these Laws of Correspondence and Analogy to investigate further the hidden nature of Deity, the universe and man. At times, however, he will need to lay aside these tools of the mind so that he may quietly wonder, and then rejoice in the loveliness of a world he is beginning to understand.

The third channel for the Mysteries, the Esoteric Group, sensitive to the incoming Aquarian influences, will continue to share the inner teachings with all who truly seek and inquire. Less than ever today can these teachings remain divorced from the affairs of practical living. Everything concerning humanity's welfare at any level can be redirected and reformed through some knowledge of the Ageless Wisdom teachings. In this the three channels for the Mysteries must wisely as well as daringly lead the way.

4.   *The Reappearance of the Christ*

"Whenever there is a withering of the law and an uprising of lawlessness on all sides, *then* I manifest Myself."

"For the salvation of the righteous and the destruction of such as do evil, for the firm establishing of the Law I come to birth age after age." *The Bhagavad Gita,* Book IV, Sutra 7, 8.

As we consider the present world conditions can we doubt that the time is near for such another manifestation?

The great clock of time cycles as marked by the celestial zodiac has indicated the hour; the "minutes" depend considerably on humanity. For through several such minutes of experience and decisions—wise or "*other*-wise"—humanity as well as each individual man and woman can learn enough to tip the scales towards an imminent approach, which means either before or very soon after the turn of our century.

From within the very heart of God (the central Mystery) there issues forth the cosmic heart-beat whereby is set the measured time-rhythm of those successive revelations through which the Love-Wisdom of God is made known to man.

The new age teachings, an intrinsic part of these revelations, are entwined within the Golden Thread which gleams with an unprecedented lustre regarding the Second Coming of the Christ. The Tibetan, the Master Djwhal Khul (as he is known today), has said more than once within his writings, and continually implies, that all his work is directed towards the preparation for this tremendous event.

He tells us that his own second Ray Ashram which is linked to the larger one of the Master Koot Hoomi (the Head of the second ray), together with the other ashrams, is engrossed in this preparation for the Coming, the first part of which is the gradual "Externalisation of the Hierarchy" among mankind. The first few in connection with the Externalisation, certain forerunners, have already made their appearance. Most of them have been unrecognised as such; a few, however, have shown unmistakable signs of being of that calibre and grade, in spite of the hampering circumstances within which they have had perforce to work.

At the time of transition from one era into another a quickening tempo is felt together with an attempted modulation into another key, the right harmonies of which belong only to the established new age conditions. For a while that which is experienced is mainly discord arising through conflict which leads up to crises through the experience of which the finer rhythms and subtler harmonies are slowly brought into being.

The Teacher himself, encompassed by these finer new age wavelengths, is preparing for his own approach to a world already responding faintly to the new energies. The "preparing of the way" is in progress, guided by the Hierarchy from behind the scenes and aided by the forerunners already in incarnation.

These are the initiates of the earlier degrees, disciples, aspirants together with forward-looking and inclusive thinkers in all departments of human living. All of these, the entire group of world servers, are drawing closer in the inner worlds in readiness for the Coming of the Lord.

The Teacher—by whatever name he will be known is immaterial—will come to ALL men. All will however by no means accept him. There will of necessity be many grades of recognition from complete acceptance down to complete rejection. His chosen personality, racial colouring, his mode of approach through the use of any modern method and contact, the new teaching he may give in fresh and unfamiliar terms; all this may meet with divers shades of either understanding and acclaim, puzzlement or with complete repudiation. The existence of many claiming to speak either as or on behalf of the Teacher is likely to test and try human perception of truth as never before. And yet, without any claim-making whatsoever (which thereby invalidates the claim), many disciples will in varying degree be "impressed" during their speech and action, or simply through radiation, when circumstances as seen from the inner side of life warrant such reinforcement.

The modern versions of "the tables of the money changers"—though these do not always deal in cash—may well once more be "overturned". There will be little respect of persons as such; but in every walk of life those who have tried their utmost to serve mankind according to their capacity will be given increased power and opportunity to serve. This is all such people would ask—if indeed they ask at all.

Above all, the Mysteries will be restored as through the new inflow of Love-Wisdom man's realisation of his relation to the WHOLE increases. Through the spiritually invigorating presence of the Teacher the three channels for the Mysteries will adopt simpler forms, vitally expressive and more revealing of deeper layers of truth of which each has been a custodian during millennia of years and through an ever moving kaleidoscope of varied circumstances. Some while before his Coming and later through his Presence the world begins to sense that spiritual renascence which is now as surely on its way as was that earlier cultural Renaissance, as it began to dissipate the mediaeval gloom—even then preparing the way for the new age which was to begin near the end of this our own century.

RECOMMENDED READING

The following books are recommended as introductions to most of the main modern presentations of the Ageless Wisdom teaching. Nearly all the authors listed have written a number of books:

Vera Stanley Alder: *The Finding of the Third Eye*
Sri Aurobindo: *The Life Divine*
Alice A. Bailey: *Initiation, Human and Solar; Letters on Occult Meditation; The Reappearance of the Christ; From Intellect to Intuition*, and other titles referred to in this book.
Foster Bailey: *The Spirit of Masonry*
Annie Besant: *A Study in Consciousness*
Paul Brunton: *The Inner Reality*
R. M. Bucke: *Cosmic Consciousness*
Buddhist Lodge: *Concentration and Meditation*
Teilhard de Chardin: *The Phenomenon of Man*
G. de Purucker: *Man in Evolution*
Hugh l'A. Faussett: *Fruits of Silence*
Joel Goldsmith: *The Infinite Way*
Manly P. Hall: *Lectures on Ancient Philosophy*
Head, Cranston et al.: *Reincarnation: an East-West Anthology*
Max Heindel: *Rosicrucian Cosmo-Conception*
R. Heywood: *The Sixth Sense*
Geoffrey Hodson: *The Kingdom of the Gods*
Humanitas: *Aum*
Raynor Johnson: *The Imprisoned Splendour*
J. Krishnamurti: *Commentaries on Living*
J. C. Leonard: *The Higher Spiritualism*
Francis Merchant: *The Golden Hoard*
Maurice Nicol: *The New Man*
Arthur Osborne: *The Axis and the Rim*
P. D. Ouspensky: *Tertium Organum*
Vera Reid: *Towards Aquarius*
Roerich: *Hierarchy*
Mouni Sadhu: *In Days of Great Peace*
Cyril Scott: *Outline of Modern Occultism*
Rudolph Steiner: *Knowledge of the Higher Worlds*
Swami Vivekananda: *Raja Yoga*
Kenneth Walker: *Only the Silent Hear*
Florence Widutis: *Yours is the Power*
W. L. Wilmshurst: *The Meaning of Masonry*
Ernest Wood: *Secret Doctrine Digest*

Training for new age

discipleship is provided

by the *Arcane School.*

The principles of the

Ageless Wisdom are

presented through esoteric

meditation, study and

service as a *way of life.*

*Write to the publishers
for information.*